The Annoying Megaphone Pigeon

By

Dwane Reads

Copyright Dwane Reads 2013

ISBN 978 0 9535 626 2 6

Piggyback Press

Email: seema@seemagillheley.com

All rights reserved. This book is copyrighted and must not be copied, reproduced, transferred, distributed, leased, licensed or publicly performed in any way except as permitted in writing by the Author.

Many thanks to editors of the following, in which some of these poems, or earlier versions, first appeared: Derby Trader, Kismaas, The words of the voice, City zine, The Derby Free, DIY Poets, Here Comes Everyone.

Printed by
Dragon Print and Design. Hitchin.

Set

1. Tongues
2. Wheelbarrow Man
   — muscle con was —
3. 4 dollar wrinkle trick
4. PUB AUCTION
5. HAPPY SHOPPING
6. BOARDERS/barriers

Poet's bit.

This book is dedicated to my children Grace and Scott.

Love you loads kids. Dad xx.

If you had of asked me about a book around the time of the John Cooper Clarke gig I would have laughed at you. That is until, "Big Bet Boy and Tales of other Crazy fools." I realized a volume of work had been constantly building; my set list kept having new stuff added regularly. So, with this in mind, I offer you my new book.

"The Annoying Megaphone Pigeon."

I have included two poems from the eighties, Arrive Dachau and Fish. Arrive was performed recently for the Holocaust Memorial Day. Fish is one of my poems that I always get asked for.

So, from the various set lists here are my poems. (An album will follow, so look out for that). Read these poems anywhere, especially places you wouldn't see a gig, Launderettes, Fast food Outlets and Taxi ranks. Or just put the kettle on, make a pot of tea and enjoy some time with my writing.

I would like you to write a poem to me after reading this book. Maybe about a character, or just about something from the book, please. This will be a new project and you are invited to contribute. You could find yourself published. A selection will be shortlisted, published and performed at a later date.

Poems to be sent to

theannoyingmegaphonepigeon@hotmail.co.uk

Forward

There is a fine line between genius and garbage; I personally veer to the genius side, although on occasions I have thought to myself why? But that is Dwane, he gets a reaction either way and doesn't care one bit what you think. The fact of the matter is he does it, travelling up and down the country performing to people who like myself get drawn in to a strange world of madness about fish in electric wardrobes and big bet boy (lend us a fiver).Tales of surrealism and life go hand in hand in Dwane's world as hopefully this book of his work will prove to you, nothing is of the radar.

I first met Dwane sometime in the 1980s when I played a gig with him when he was in a band called the huba buba tea company of tibet an off the wall band who played with a washing line of pants put across the stage. I also watched his art work progress, sometimes completely bizarrely, like the time in Derby he put hundreds of old pennies in the street spelling words out, nobody took any notice and most were just kicked around the precinct. Dwane also busked on a shopping trolley and made the papers on many occasion, for his off the wall antics, but it was poetry that inspired him and he would often be found performing in a pub that didn't have the right crowd to appreciate his work, not that it bothered him he would just carry on regardless with an enthusiasm that is not matched by many. Dwane took a break from poetry in the 1990s to raise a family, but rekindled his love of writing and performing and in 2011 came back to perform at a gig at the Flowerpot in Derby, as support to John Cooper Clarke.

Since that day he has never looked back and has developed a loyal following of his work and new supporters, who like me, wonder what half of it is all about whilst appreciating the genius that is Dwane Reads.   Johnny Vincent.

Words from others

Dwane is a true social surrealist: he manages to be hard hitting and completely off the wall at the same time. Well worth a listen.

(Attila the Stockbroker)

Often funny often poignant, always uncompromising Dwane Reads' poems take you by surprise. These poems are full of characters you need to meet and places you need to visit.

(Helen Mort. Spire Writes Chesterfield)

The everyday made fascinating through the Dwane Reads filter system, creative imaginative and able to hold the audience's attention and fascination.

(Eagle Spits)

Thematically favouring 'kitchen Sink' Poetry.

(Gary Longden. Lichfield Poets)

Dwane is the Dennis the Menace of the poetry Circuit – loud, mischievous and full of surprises. A "must see" artist.

(Gary Carr, Spoken Worlds)

All life is unconventional and Dwane Reads is the perfect poet to capture it.

(Mal Dewhirst. Staffordshire poet Laureate 2012/13)

contents page

page	poem/ image
2	set list
3	title page
4	set list
5	poet's bit.
6	forward with pic.
7	forward
8	contents
9	contents
10	contents / Dwane Reads performing live
11	Wheelbarrowman
12	abstract voices/ set list
13	tonuges
14	fish/ flyer
15	gulls
16	four dollar wrinkle trick
17	Dwane Reads performing live
18	Dumb down the nation
19	comics not funny anymore
20	call 'em love bites
21	jam wars
22	you could hang for that
23	when the giant came to town
24	still wanna be in ? / the journey
25	men that sing
26	why do I attract nutters ?
27	unmask the wrestler
28	the boffin wants to get me
29	gateman
30	bite your bottom lip
31	meat parade / muted
32	Dwane Reads with speech bubble
33	bikini bodies / blame culture
34	borders barriers flags
35	food bank
36	the annoying megaphone pigeon
37	big bet boy
38	new shoes
39	I wanna / Line drawing

40	cash for hurts
42	oddball
43	dinosaurs. we like dinosaurs
44	metal bird
45	plastic paddy
46	bella
47	food salvage trip
48	growing older (remembering)
49	leaflets contributed to ill health
50	who is reading what (blog)
51	happy shopping
52	Helen
53	translucent teardrops
54	turtles verse piracy (heroes and villans)
55	could you be a clown
56	don't steal Malcolm Henry or Paul
58	toyshop lockin
59	the big I am
60	wake up to what's going on around you
61	Dwane Reads performing live
62	belt
63	bert
64	time taken up doing nothing
65	bus clippy
66	dolly
67	he wrote it in pen
69	Dwane Reads performing live with Tezza punky prawn on stage. Attack of the killer Prawn
70	aliens lament
71	hero was always villainous / air swimming
72	just past my die by date
73	I had dreamed of vampire / tell me
74	south bay trash
75	wishing
76	wonder boy and the pig
77	Dwane Reads performing live. Poop trees
78	pub auction
79	Dwane Reads performing live. The shoe queen
80	comic book anti hero
81	quirky little hook
82	R5
83	shops gone
84	Dwane Reads Performing live

85	arrive Dachau (death)
86	keep away from me
87	you're fed your life's shit
88	drunk
89	your not eighteen anymore
90	druggie on the roof
92	flyer
93	muston conway
94	unicorn tales
95	Dwane Reads on the railway platform. Thanks page
97	now you write a poem
98	Dwane Reads

Wheelbarrow man (inspired by chicken roundabout in bungay)

Wheelbarrow Man trundles towards the Island
Ritual like
With Chuck Chuck to feed the abandoned
Only a handful remain due to a cowardly senseless cull
Someone knows who did it….no answers yet

His double distance round trip clocks ten
In miles not minutes
He's fit for his seventy plus years
His hands and arms strain whilst he masters balance
With a firm grip on those handles

The tops of his Wellington boots quiver as he walks
Occasionally scraping his heels
It's all routine now …Every step

There resettled in the middle of a roundabout
On an island on a roundabout
The smell of freedom to roam at will
Release the birds its feeding time

Abstract Voices

Sat on a bus
Talking into a cell phone
Faceless voices
Talking back

There are forty conversations
But, not with the persons sat opposite
Or next to you
Just faceless voices talking back
Into a cell phone

Tongues

Cal a wacka ma keelie mar cumba ma kor
Cal a wacka ma keelie mar cumba ma kor
Cal a wacka ma keelie mar cumba ma kor
Tongues
And I don't know what it means
It just came to me
I repeated it
Rhythm Chant mantra
It felt right
Good
No understanding yet
You know it's calming, forthright exhilarating
Easy on the tongue
No understanding
But, as in tongues
Just let it flow

Cal a wacka ma keelie mar cumba ma kor
Cal a wacka ma keelie mar cumba ma kor
Cal a wacka ma keelie mar cumba ma kor

Fish

Fish in electric wardrobe swim
Watch their eyes and fins
Fish in electric wardrobes
Watch them swim

Gulls

Gulls hover
In cross winds
Like fighter pilots
Over chips and batter
Hear their call
In high pitched screech
Perched waiting
Peck eat

Four dollar wrinkle trick (the face mask)

Mums four dollar wrinkle trick
Before and after
Arrrgh!
It's
Arrrgh!
It's
I don't want to know the secret
Go go away
It's horrible
Take off the mask
Take off the mask
Please
Clowns can scare people
Aliens too
But that stuff on your
Four dollar wrinkle trick

Dumb down the nation

You own the hospitals you own the schools
You read the papers treated as fools
Dumb down the nation is this what you want?
Apathy said, "take it easy man, can't be bothered,
No action plan."
You've lost the hunger, no belly to fight
No reason to complain only comply
Relax and chill out no questions why

Dumb down the nation is all that you get
No questions nor answers are asked or set

Stand to attention do as you're told
You might get a pension if you live to be old
But only enough to merely exist because you never took action or tried to resist

You follow the leader never break rank all of your savings safe in the bank
Dumb down the Nation who's in control
Who set the agenda do what you're told
Don't teach them to read
No nothing at all….
Wide screen telly and media control

Dumb down the nation is all what we've got
Unless we take action
WE'VE LOST THE LOT………..
Dumb down the nation never break rank
Take what you're given…
Manners…Thanks!

Comics not funny anymore

The comics on the telly are not funny anymore
Like the one's we had in film and radio years ago
Their boring and predictable stage managed without a craft
If put to sea they'd drown even sat upon a raft
If given call up papers they'd avoid the draft

Oh our comics are not funny anymore

They seem to think there witty
But are the audiences playing their part
Can you see the man at the side of the stage?
With a placard reading LAUGH
See if he wasn't there it would be silent like a morgue
So go on laugh again you robot you cyborg

There's nothing about the dumb blonde
Or the fat chick
The copper the robber
The paddy said to Mick
How do you get your material?
What is it that makes you tick?

Oh our comics are not funny anymore

Are you frightened you might offend?
Be written out of a pilot
That will be dropped in the end
You only got your part due to that "relationship with a friend"
Because we are not laughing just slow hand clapping

Turning that radio dial
Switch the telly off… for a while
Those entire rave reviews are now yesterday's news
Oh our comics are not funny anymore.

Call 'em love bites

Call 'em love bites
More like dog bites hanging from a neck
She's reeking of skunkweed…I was almost sick
The floor is littered with paper and cans
An' clothes just stepped out of where they had stood
How long I don't know

I was offered a coffee but I turned it down
The sink unit was encrusted with dirt
A browning green
Piles of newspapers wet from a constant dripping
From the ceiling above
Put me right off a drink
A cup was dug out of a mound of clothes washing….
Piled up with carrier bags of crushed red bull and larger cans
No thank you I'll pass
I sat down in the comfy chair this was the lounge
Scattered on the floor was a pile of magazines
I don't think the carpet had ever been cleaned
Never mind hoovering

There was a smell of damp and something rotten
Maybe a combination of the ceiling dripping the laundry or both
But the rotten smell…that was BAD ODOUR
They had obviously gotten used to it
But for a visitor
It hit me
I've got good smellers the best of times
I am out of here

Jam wars

Racing down the 52
Passing me passing you
Pulling out movin' through
Music blasting
Who are you?
Moving forward getting through

Zig zag zigging
Zig zag zogging
Zig zag zigging
Zig zag zigging

In and out and in and out
And in an out again
Along the 52

Pulling your long faces
Pulling long faces

And hand gestures
And hand gestures
And hand gestures
Not an inch gained

In Jam Wars.

You could hang for that

Ding dong bell
Your goanna go to hell
For the crimes you're committing
Putting boys in the well

We know it's your profession
And your tasks are done well
But there are some things you mustn't
Never ever ever tell

Tom Dick Harry promised food drink light
Giving warmth and comfort on a death cold night
Encourage not to question, just eat whilst warm
Rest up; get some sleep child till early morn'

They gave the boy the porter for its strength was strong
Plus a little drop of poison that would help him along
His head went a spinning He became very sick
The well dresser criminals played a horrid horrid trick

They placed a rope around him binding his arms to his wrist
And lowered him down as he mumbled with a twist
As he dangled his way down an iced mossed wall
If the cold doesn't kill you the deep water will

Left him submerged dangling in the cold watered ice
Whilst they returned to an ale house to last out the night
Returned in the morn to retrieve him dead
Cutting off his hands and feet disposing of his head

Off to the doctor the madman on the hill
For a gold piece of sovereign promised at will
Bring me a body in the name of science
Bring me a body in the name of science
Bring me a body in the name of science
I will pay you well

When the giant came to town

They were all put out of business when the giant came to town
Who offered jobs a plenty for someone they could trust
With a reference and a smile
Soon there'll be no local shops
It didn't take a while
First, we lost the newsagents, the hardware fancy dress
And as they lowered prices, small business fell into a mess
They called it competition and challenge as they might
But, with their buying power, only they could win the fight
Ample free car parking to help you fill your boot
Whilst other local business faltered…
But they didn't give a hoot!
The giant supermarket wants to swallow you whole
And if you let them do it, they will conquer and control
You haven't any transport. Then use our clean free bus
We can get you there and back with the minimum of fuss
To the twenty first century cathedral
All gleaming shiny bright
With its neatly stacked shelves like solders on parade
Ready for battle to commence
But did they ever visit? And try their merchandise
Or like the others moan and pass by once or twice
So much for local custom so much for being loyal
Thanks for nothing locals protest when the giant's plans unveiled
Hypocrite locals swim their crocodile tears
Never visited local shops that stood there for years
A memory, nostalgic maybe you'll read about
When it's long closed down
Thanks for nothing mate…it's gone
Should have used it when it was there anybody got any junk?
There's a charity shop opening in the precinct

Still wanna be in?

So you wanna join our gang eh?
Yeh
Um…. your gonna have to let the fat kid fall on you
Full on
Face to face from standing that's the deal
Still wanna be in?
Get Mannie
Go get Mannie
He is having his dinner
Surprise surprise
Go tell him we need him and with some urgently
Someone wants to be in
Minnie said, "He will be out in a minute.
But, can he change things around a little?
Instead of face to face
From standing he wants to jump
Off the wall as long as we hold the enunciated
By their arms…whilst they are laying down more impact
BOOM
Like wrestlers in wwf
Still wanna be in?

The journey

Eat up the garbage
Hurry
Get the magic crow
To fly where the mermaid princess is
Use your knowledge of colour and shade to guide you

Men that sing

Singing on the terraces or alone in the shower
Barbershop quartet a Welsh male voice choir
Lifting the spirit's a feeling of one
Encouraging triumphant the joy of the song

Music Hall hecklers transformed into chants
Sea shanty local tales whilst Morris men dance
Pub entertainers blast out on the mic
Our favourite songs on a cold weekday night

Striking men gathered from Pit Land and Sea
After marching in protest on empty
With their voices strong unions sang as one
Demanding rights, better pay for the plenty

Men singing solo duets or in crowds
Whilst their team are hopelessly defeated
Muted

Why do I attract Nutters?

Why do I attract Nutters?
It's always the bloody same
Have I got a f*****g arrow
Sticking from my head?
Free parking for the insane

There must be a f*****g arrow
Poised above my head
Like a neon glowing halo
Reading : kick 'im till he's dead

Why do I attract Nutters?
Here's one on the phone
Why don't you want to talk to me?
Just leave me the f**k alone

Why do I attract Nutters?
It's always the bloody same
I spoke to you a lifetime ago
Remember…

Unmask the wrestler

That's what you come for
You've paid your money
For some action…
Dangerous
Tense
Excitable
Action

Somebody's going to go down
Somebody's goanna take a fall and dive intentionally or not
It could be even the ref…tonight
In his black and white chiffon shirt
Squealing like a pig for his mom ma
As he crashed, smashed down.

So who you goanna side with?
Simpletons?
Losers?
Villains and bad'uns

Make yourself feel better and shout
When they unmask the wrestler
You notice the local butcher
Protesting defiant shamed.
Smashed to the canvas

Hold if you can to a count of three
Forearm smash leads to a Boston crab…submit…submit…

The Boffin wants to get me

My time is up I've got to run
That Boffin son of mine
His perverse idea of fun
You see He toiled for a while

In his room at night underneath his bed
By head strapped searchlight
He's programmed downloaded adapted switched
Circuit boards wires…everything's mixed

My son's mobile phone has grown in size
It's me who is hunted…surprise surprise
The reality of which has me terrified
Time for me to hide

I must run a distance out of his glare
Just to get away…anywhere
I might never come back would I be missed?
Ray gun laser vapour has me galloping with a twist

Where are the saboteurs
To throw this monster off scent
Whilst the Boffin tracks my movements
Via GPS navigator…
Infer- red night vision Google finder

Miles across country in all weathers I have run
Avoiding radiation tariffs from the mast
Escaping dangers its radio waves of rage
Where is this monster hosted?
From where are these games played?
Via GPS navigator…
Infer red night vision Google finder

Can we not play Lurkie Lurkie instead?

Gateman

There used to stand a factory over there
That's what they will say
When the build comes…houses
Unaffordable shoe boxed…new
Traditions, memories banter…gone
For now a solitary gateman
Watching cars
Make or colour counts this in the rain
Previously it was humans
Being dog walked, in the rain
Wishing he could escape
His shift of boredom
The only working man on our estate
No hooter blast
No shift exchange
No future here
For ever changed
Just a gateman in residence
Watching over silence of abandoned production lines
Where 40,000 livelihoods once toiled
Listen out for ghost, can you sense them?
Eerie, Haunted, dull.
Has you shuddering
As barriers about to jolt closed
Trains are on their way
They keep time here
Collecting numbers
Scribbling rhythmically onto paper scrapes
Then write up into best
From inside a building he now patrols

Bite your bottom lip

Bite your bottom lip
But not all the way through
That's physical pain
It will heal overtime
What chance has he got?

Thirty eight to one they're all on him
Some he doesn't even know
But they are joining in
Going along with it
He just wants them all
Just f**k off won't yeh
I say just let him escape from it all
Do something else let him escape.

Meat parade

Meat parade out on our streets
Meat parade in clubs & bars
They get hooked up and bleed one another dry
Our city is awash with suited and booted
And hair done up to the nines
Fake tans and jewellery clanker the streets
Can't walk in the high heels that cost a tidy sum
Just wait while I piss away tonight up a wall
Can I see you again?

Muted

Stitched up with invisible thread
The needle dangles from bloody lips
All swallow sore with nothing to say
Just a grunt came out no dialect there
Muted silent healing wound
Unable to bite your way through

Bikini bodies

Gym fit for magazines
Lifted...pulled...tucked
Go on. Under the knife haggard looking
No mirrors hang here
Bikini bodies' gym fit for magazines
Lifted...pulled...tucked
Be confident in your own skin
Not an object
The look you seek is Photoshop

Blame culture

Blame culture
It wasn't my fault
Blame culture
Point and accuse
Blame culture
It isn't any use
Blame culture
Allowed carry on
Blame culture
Who's done wrong?

Borders barriers flags

Borders barriers flags of nations
Keep you different segregation
Walls built high to keep you in
To protect you from yourselves
Caged like animals in a human zoo
Controlled, told what to do
CCTV track your movements
For our government spies

Build bridges, not stocks nor gallows
Don't allow those hungry dogs their feast
Or it will be you dreadlocked vegetarian
Thrown in the pit to the pigs
Accepted, explained as justification
An example set for all
You challenged with too many questions
Now Stood blindfolded awaiting the call

Fire!

Food Bank

Twenty first century this is the UK
In our towns and cities food banks hidden away
They're springing up across the country
At a rate of two a week
Helping people…who only want to eat

Collect and redistributing food thrown away
That's out of date or gone bad by only one day
Pick the green out the bread have it as toast
Cut at damaged fruit for the child who likes it most

Eat at ten or four' o' clock, but only once a day
Enduring hunger pains that continue through the week
We have a food bank here if your hungry come and seek

They've come in four by fours and vans disappeared like ghost
Making out how needy a 'Genuine Case'?
But left on hearing 'assessment' coupled with 'investigate'
Different circumstances desperate people wait

Carry bags of handouts containing varieties of food
Unlike a grabbin's of a ram raiders smash
Everything is used here it's shared not for cash
Donations accepted in any quantity
Local businesses give a ways donations by the score
Difficulties in these times to recognise the poor

The sincere offer gratitude and with their families break bread
Whilst the less scrupulous see this as a saving
Drive to Ikea and buy a bed…Bastards

The Annoying Megaphone Pigeon

Don't feed the birds
There's a fine in it for you if you do
Seventy quid plus cost
Don't feed the birds
They don't want to hear their call
Plus the mess is costing
That's the reality the cost
There are supposed patrols
Pigeon feeder catchers like unmarked police cars
No flashing blue nee- nar light
Oh, no plain clothed
How much does that cost?
More than those nets, you see here and there
Above the eye line of our towns and cities
Cooing
Being chased in circles by young children Arrrgh
Who like the commotion?
The lift off
The sound of the fluttering of wings
Forget the food
Get out of here and fly
Moments later returning
Dive bomb style to pick peck
At crust on the ground
Rained on Soggy wet
But a tasty beak filler for the brave
Swoop in
Weathered bronze familiar silent
Streaked in white green yellowed shite
From head hand shoulder
Nothing is sacred here left in the open
If only they could silence
Gather and cull
Transform to wood or stone
Stuff then display
Leave a line of crumb as you sit
Rub fingers together between bread
Until those fingers meet
Feed the birds
Defy the fine
Just don't get caught

Big Bet Boy

53 Still at home
The big bet boy
Lend us a fiver
53 he likes his lunch
His mam made it
Triangles with a slice of cheese
You know how I like it,
Now get it done!
Mammy Mammy, have you got any money?
I've spent mine
Gambled it away on the three 15 at Ayr.
But it was a dead cert'
(I tell you)
Fell and broke its neck at the last fence.... oh disaster!
53, still at home
The big bet boy
Lend us a fiver.
He just been given the rent to pay
He thought...He'd be up...You know...
Bit for the weekend...I'LL pay, yah....when I've got it
53...still at home
Big bet boy lend us a fiver.
And as they run for home
It's the big bet boy lend us a fiver
Sitting in silence
With his mother's rent
Followed by no favourite tea
Telly gone and up to a week
What am I going say...
He's won some back
He's won some back
But not enough!
53 and still at home
The big bet boy lend us a fiver
He's beggin' me
He's beggin' me
He's lost again
Down a monkey
I'LL pay later...I'LL be up
You know... Bit extra for the weekend...
I'LL pay... next race.

New shoes

In summer time, the sun melted the tarmac Squidgy soft
Rather than damage those new patent leather shoes
She walked barefoot
Gathering chippings of asphalt between her toes
Stride and stroll along the road without a care in the world
This is how it should be
Fingers grip the straps of the newly bought…deemed priceless

I wanna

I wanna be running in the park playing airplanes
Not a care in the world
I wanna be catching Sticklebacks, putting 'em in jars
To watch their wriggling
I wanna be giggling, howling with laughter
About something so funny it hurts
I wanna be a good Dad, have my children love me
Hold my wife by the hand, occasionally kiss and hug me
I wanna be all those things and more, two times two equals four
I wanna be the Leprechaun at the end of the rainbow
When it all works out, like in films that make you cry
Yet, you never intended to, let on
And I looked at you looking at me, we're both weeping
I wanna just say how glad I am to be with you.

Cash for hurts

Be careful of what u read in ads
As priceless objects can demand
A premium taken underhand
With no questions…Mister?

Some family stuff sold as seen
It's dating back before the queen
Don't ring back asking for more
The brother has habit

Take the advert form the wall
Mixed amongst the bikes and chairs
Mobile hairdressers and the betterwear
Read again in disbelief and places
Folded neatly in your palm

Cash for hurts…a real treat
Phone this number be discreet
Local to the area

I knew what I did was wrong
When made the visit
Only once mind… only once

Cash for hurts the hacksaws wrote
Its ages since our last approach
They don't come along often
But when they do… when they do
It…s   wonder…fully   ex…ci…ting
How do you do?
Waxed wooden box that smells
Of soup or musty shop
Awaits investigation placed on a
Starched stretched doily
Held together under key and lock
Carved and made to conceal what?
Kept in a solution
Hidden over years of time
Viewed only in private
Like a stolen…masterpiece
Open to offers best price secures.

Its fingers and ears that I collect…I was told
How much for yours?
Don't run the doors are bolted
And windows firmly shut
The cash for hurts money
Take it…take it… it's yours
Place the additions on the table
We soon will have them cut
Too late to retract on the deal
It's been already struck
Already been….
Cash for hurts…a real treat
Phone this number be discreet local to the area

Oddball

They said he was and oddball
Lonesome and queer
Never shall you talk to him
Let him get near
If he does approach you
Better run an' hide
These are the stereotypes some
Mothers had guides

Always be suspicious always on your guard
Never trust anyone
It isn't very hard
He doesn't look like us
So always cross the road
The language is different
Cannot crack the code
Some said he was foreign,
Others mentioned gay
If you see 'im in street's...nearby
Don't greet... run away
Remember...a little different
Strange... another way
Careful does it in ignorance
Eat and eat away
Rot and maybe fester
Leave alone today
Cross the streets and bow your head
And hope it goes away.
Do we have to have this happen?
Are you gonna act this way?
Be responsible for your actions
Can we act another way?
Do we hold a hand of friendship?
And offer to break bread
Or turn away in anger
With threats of you are dead...

Dinosaurs. We like Dinosaurs

Plastic moulded textured figure
How we practiced your name
Tri -o - ter - o - tops -a- thingy
Like learning a language
A new language
Displaced jigsaw bones
Held by fine wire
Xylophone like
Don't touch fragile
Walk round under
Gaze in wonder
We like Dinosaurs

Metal Bird

Metal bird, metal bird brings mushrooms to the sky
Apparition told the children picking potatoes out the dirt
To prepare themselves now whilst she protects the earth
People walk masked shielded from the sun
As evolution starts, again a new dawn has begun
Zero hour counting no clocks only moon
Track your movements from the stars
You will be home soon
Drink snow it's melting safe to quench your thirst
Barren landscapes livestock sculptured into dirt
Metal bird, metal bird brings mushrooms to the sky
Prophecy to the children only they listened

No one else survived

Plastic paddy

The seasons are changing
Yes indeed it's, early march
The daffodils are uprooted and strewn, across the grass
The plastic paddy lies there pissed his shirt all torn
Revealing the badge of the three lions
He's so proudly had tattooed
You never heard NEVER SURRENDER
The arm could not salute
Because of a different environment it's shoes worn rather than boots
He likes it a day for a piss up a feckin' all day sess'h
Wasting all of his money on Guinness and made up stew
Today you see he's Irish top of the morning to you
Plastic paddy go back crawl into your slum
For tomorrow is another day
And I know what you'll become
English mate and proud of it
BRITANIA ROOLS
Why do they come over here always on the take?
You see its back to normal now, I am English mate
The green plastic paddy is it someone we should shun?
Like an unwanted plastic toy figure of a solider with his gun
I'm glad it's only once a year and in a day it's gone
Keep St Patrick's Day for the Irish…not everyone
It seems to be devalued. Hijacked in fact
Due to big businesses trying hype to sell the craick
Plastic paddy here again joining in but without a soul
Making up the number on a senseless parade
10% Irish 90% homemade waving a tricolor held tightly in the hand
with the other he would beat you if you came from foreign lands
Plastic paddy's happy what a marvellous day
It's great to be Irish
If only for a day.

Bella

Life
Somewhere is all set out
It should be labelled not to choose
As you don't know what's to come
That's the journey the unknown
Take Bella with her good bit of fortune
She believed she had won the lottery well as good as for her
Just to get that council flat over there on the ground floor
How she danced once inside her two young children
Each one from a different relationship
Strained uncompromising and difficult
But it is how you cope with things and Bella coped
She was strong
So she brought the kids up in that place
With its open space it was like having your own private park
Just outside your front door
Bella move on in life with a public house
The one on the corner
She don't own it it's a renter
But the flat above is sublet and she gets by
When she is all done, she is just moving across the road
Into the old folks home
If it's still there that is
She hopes to do the old folk thing
With some family visits from time to time
Trips out if possible
Whilst growing old

Food salvage trip

Early morning raids from the co-op's bin finished
When they knowingly erected a fifteen foot fence
For meat joints perishable thrown into a skip
So now it's further hunting to obtain stuff to eat
More mileage if wanting those little treats

Accosted by coppers as they flashed lights
He was told not asked to show inside his bag
That he so tightly clasped -they thought was swag
It's mouldy meat bread and soup stuff I can't afford
Not stolen beer and fags or a house break in hoard

Rummaging through dustbins large Supermarket skips
Out at night till early morning on food salvage trips
Don't patronise me with pity this stuffs been thrown away
Unwanted neglected fit for landfill some would say
Find me around the back of shops
As I walk the silent streets
It's only that I'm hungry can't afford to eat

Growing older (remembering)   (This is for Derby Band Mr Wolf)

Feel my skin
Its wrinkles outnumber the memories
Held in my head
Growing old remembering
Still remembering
On constant rewind
Growing older
What have I got to look forward to?
Grandchildren
Meals on wheels
Care homes
Put the radio on
Wasn't that the Clash?
…Tommy Gun

Leaflets contributed to ill health

Golden fry
Pizza chips loads of pies
With photographs that resemble goo
It does not look too good for you
That's the leaflet that came through my letterbox today

With no health warnings… get in on the act
Before the government's plans are cracked
To have junk food outlets on all estates
On all the corners in the towns

Amongst the dwindling shop parades
With new funeral parlours moved into old pubs
Chemist with their slow death drugs

Is there a master plan to kill us all?
Before we reach a certain age?
So science fiction becomes science fact
What age please for your heart attack?

No room here madam...sorry chap
In take only those who can afford
Others will be left to rot lonely silent forgot
Social care has been closed down, far too expensive to the town
Unemployment might be up, there has to be certain cuts

It's golden fry, chippy bus, out on the streets tempting us
Edible nightmares …kill us slow
Take away the benefit cash
From the eaters seen as trash
Is it because they cannot cook? Can't be bothered?
Don't give a f**k
Feed 'em this and with a bit of luck, no need for further health care!

Golden fry, opening time, free delivery, phone hunger line.
Golden fry, opening soon, opposite funeral parlour
(Used to be star and garter) Remember?

Who's reading what (blog?)

You write a Blog to yourself
Spending hours souring stuff
Translations on your own
Yes, I am sure you've messed it up
You write an argument to yourself
About communicating words
That nobody reads
Zero comments in the box
Yet still you have the need
To upload
Types again resize

Wasting time within the net
But you don't realise the clock
Who is reading who about who about what
Too much information whilst nothing is being done
Reading blog's about blog's telling how blog's should be blogged

Happy shopping

It's like this
I've spent the best part of an hour
In a place I didn't actually want to be
But it had to be done shopping always does.
Anyway, I'm at the till
Well almost someone's in front
I've pulled up with a trolley, half full the usual
Bog roll… bread …salad stuff
Etc. Etc. ready to place on the belt
I'm reaching in taking out reaching in
When I'm interrupted by Mrs. assume
"I'll just go in front of you, I've only a few items and I am paying in cash"
As she moved forward to push in I quickly retorted
"Join the queue" I uttered it something in me just uttered it
"But I'm paying in cash"
The tone of her voice was liken to that of a Roller coaster ride
Mrs. assume with her scarecrow hair those blinking eyes
Maybe she did this when cross or just not getting her way
Join the queue
Instructions came from just one finger
Marvellous…what power
I quickly turned leaning over my trolley
She can repeat that to the back of my head I thought to myself
And she did, but more mumbled than before
Meanwhile
I am placing shopping into the trolley
I take my stuff and start bagging
Reaching in bagging up Reaching in bagging up
When slap bang in front of my mush
"It didn't take long did it"?
The twisted features of Mrs. assume
In my face and smug with it
Whilst I am reaching in bagging up reaching in bagging up
That must have really got under her skin
"What's her problem"? Another shopper asked
"She had to join the queue" I replied with a smile
Whilst Mrs. assume accompanied by her purchases
Mumbled her way outside the store

Happy shopping!

Helen

Come on
Grab some clothes
Shower…Ready…out of here
Let's hit the Town (so to speak)
Be together
Talk…laugh…chew the fat…
Over coffee…or a beer
It's your call
Even the silence between us is good
And I am all made up
Just to be with you (Helen)
To look at you
Hear you, touch you, hold you
Even the silence between us is good.

Translucent Teardrops

It rained translucent teardrops from a giants' eye
Causing repeated rainbow arches to snap across the skies
Encrusted stripes faded on wall and window sill
Squeezed out tube from middle like incontinent dribbled waste
As substance poured custard like flooding towns beneath
Townsfolk took their kaleidoscopes' and peering with an eye
Twisty twisted patterns danced before a monochrome sky

Turtles verse Piracy (Heroes and villains)

Ninjas versus pirates centuries apart
Trained in the skills of mixed martial arts
From storm sewers hidden deep beneath our feet
Treasures of lost merchandise swashbucklers seek

Cereal box back toy patch for an eye
Secrets on trade cards coin scratched away
Logoed torn clothing emblazed with jewels
Sold to the masses as must haves'

Teenage mutant Turtles our Heroes in a half shell

Ninjas battle Pirates the reward being gold
Via video pixilation so the story unfolds
Raise Jolly Roger skull and bones
Prepare for attack the defeated will hang
Switch on…let battle commence

Could you be a clown?

Could you be a clown?
Scale ladders run tumble making it look as if it was effortless
You're not young forever you know
Could you be a clown travelling endlessly?
I suppose its routine you've gotten used to
Once proud travelling circus now rid of its animals
Moving into the twentieth century, its press statement said
More trouble with protesters more likes
Replaced with motorcycles daring crappy stunts
Who wants that?

Don't forget the clowns they are the joke
Their antics distract the setting up of the next act or the main event
They are all that is left of the circus…tickets please

Clowns don't work alone not real clowns
In groups with their routine of pink slime custard and confetti
If health and safety hasn't ruled them out yet
Smell my flower whoops are you wet?
Could you be a clown?

Paint your face run the ring night after night
Keeping up the pretence that everything is honky dory
The fun never stops here honk honk
Audience big or small you can't buy laughter
It's hard sometimes you have to make it happen even if youngsters fear you
You're feeling trapped but you have done it for so long this is all you know
So pick up your props
Check the mirror one last time
Adjust costume because you're on

Could you be a clown?

Don't steal Malcolm Henry or Paul

Don't want your garden gnome liberationist
Stealing us from our homes
Taken on faraway trips
Whilst the others are left alone
Wrapped up in a rucksack
Amongst your smelly clothes
Then photographed by landmarks
With the evidence sent home

Stealing gnomes is silly
Have you no respect? What about my owners
They are upset …yet …distressed
I was stolen at the weekend
Will I ever return back?
Or shall I wait 'till I am damaged
Loss of paint, a hairline crack.

I bet the photographs are not of Loughborough or Burton in fact
When do you think I'll go home?
Gnome-napper, well….REACT!
I want my lawn to reside on
Not to be taken on a road trip
I could touch plant life with my magic
In the garden where I once lived
Causing flowers to open and blossom
And butterflies to drift
But now I am stuck in departure lounges or taxis and lifts

You know I'd make a placard
But you see…I cannot write
I am just a common garden gnome
I can fish… but cannot fight
I've had to put up with nonsense
And your boring solitude
Not exactly the person
For a holiday trip I'd choose
Don't launch me like a rocket man
Be calm and place me down
There appears to be a prankster
In the gardens of our town
In the middle of the night

Stealing garden gnomes
I am a great British tradition
And our gardens…are our homes

I don't want your
Garden gnome liberation action
I just want to be left alone
Ceramic bearded and silent
No fishing rod in hand
Weathered with a garden
Return me home
I demand.

Toyshop lock in

The killer mutts played dice hoping any better than a four
Would win a jackpot better than bones… honestly
Ask a police officer he is patrolling the aisles right now
Thinking to himself, he has all the authority over toy soldiers,
superheroes and Brat dolls in the bargain bin with last year's
wannabes.

Go two up and ride croggie around the store
No one's home. So Pull wheelies do some stunts
Parkour over the top of shop displays and between the roof spaces

The board games wish for only to be played
Selling at a rate of three for two
The fix of a parlour table awaits
With laughter, gasp and calls of cheating.

The big I am

Pretend to be a hard boy until you get hurt
Falling to your knees rolling in the dirt
Call out for mummy as a left hook swings
Think of better times and happier things
Curl up tightly with arms to protect
Until the kicking stop he's a horrible wreck

Scrunched up messed up
Scrabbling ball
Thought he was a hard man
Now he takes a fall
Should have kept his mouth shut
The big I am
Now he's off to hospital in the Ambulance van

Wake up to what's going on around you

Pacify the people Keep them sheep like
In their pen move them when it suits
Feed 'em holidays with familiar film sets
Allow the winning of televisions and cars to be tax-free
Encourage more to enter

Can it not be blamed on free dailies?
Most mainstream a twenty minute read
Celebrity entertainment news
Give them what they think they want

Make the minimum wage the national wage
Don't tell anyone just allow it to happen
Suspend funding for the arts again don't tell them
Just post, your application was unsuccessful this time

Close pubs having links with trade unions
Stop the gatherings that's where they talk
Bring in compulsory purchase orders take control
Break up their community close down the factory
Tell them here is a payoff
Take the family to Disney
We can get your services cheaper aboard…sorry

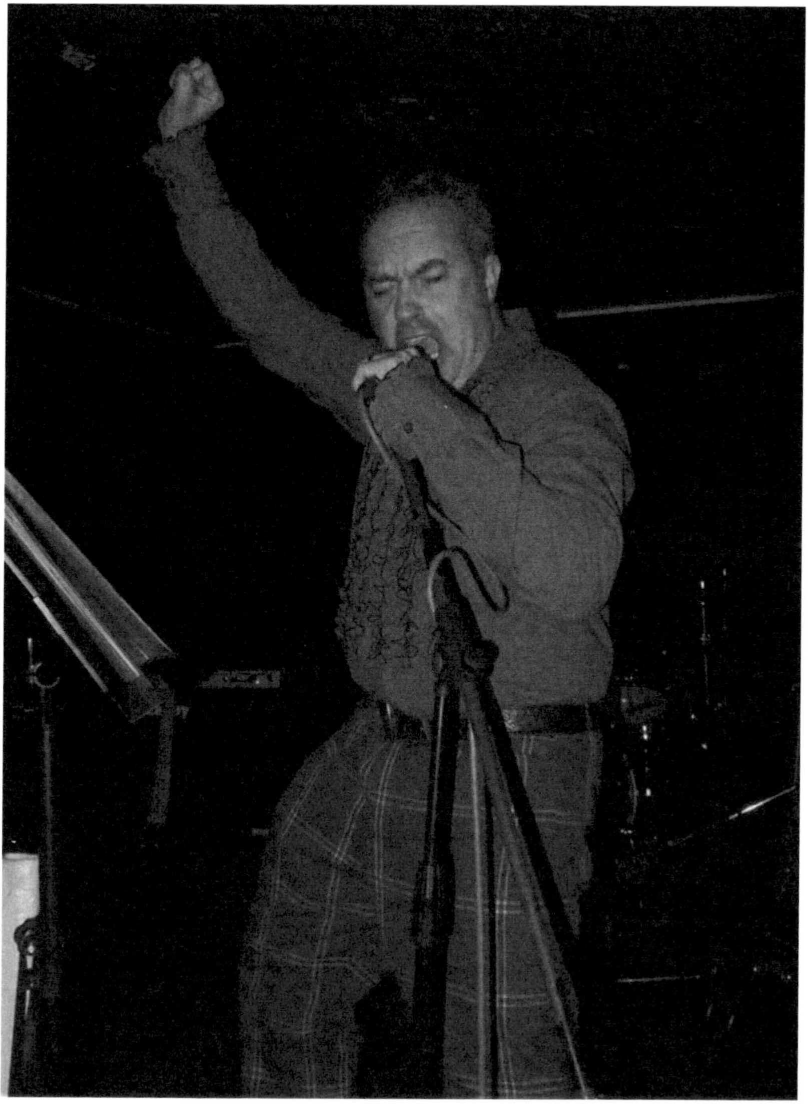

Belt

Leaders Leaders Wheelers and Dealers
Profit Makers Bonus takers
Painful steps means job losses
And I haven't got a belt to tighten
Have you saved for your retirement?

Save, save, put some by with what?
I can only manage to exist

You want us to work beyond seventy five
Whilst you in the trough drink and dine
Put everything on works account
Massage the figures cut out the fat
Take the profits up the stakes
Wipe clean all usual mistakes down to human error

Work find, work it will keep you off the street
Help you afford a belt
NOW…Tighten and swing

Bert

Here's a little story about a bloke named Bert
He don't want me to tell yah
Coz if he hears it he'll get hurt
See Bert he met a Lady thought she was very nice
So much so he fell in love thought this could be his wife
She moved into his mothers
When she found no mother there
She wanted to order furniture
Put up wallpaper here and there

Bert he didn't want to
The cost gave him a fright
But Anne Marie said come here Bert
I'll give you something nice
So Bert got his presents of cardinal delights
And Anne Marie the wallpaper
Coz she wanted it to be right

But you see that's not the end of it
In fact it was the start
It leads to more expenditure
In the end a broken heart
Next it was the carpet to match those patterned walls
Followed by the furniture and expensive paintings in the hall

The cash flow was like a river and I'd say it ran
This women seems to have a hold of Bert the single man
But he never sensed an issue when this all began
Yet looking from the outside everyone else can

But who'd the heart to tell him coz he seemed mighty fine
When you're not the player but the one that's being played
You might not like the sounds of rumors so your actions get delayed
He always got his "presents "but recently they've stopped
She was cruel and heartless to inform him he was a flop…in bed
Taken for his money taken for a twat
Nothing left of finances…anything ever last
Gone but not forgotten …house trashed in rage
Heartless selfish bast**d gone
Sorry son you've been played.

Time taken up doing nothing

Fed all this shit via Sky TV
The newspaper groups with their slant on society
Coupons giveaways they're all in cahoots
Rush down the paper bin in your imitation ugg boots
Hope to find the token number five or was it six
You missed for a weekend out of season at Butlins
Where it rains when you are pissed

Check your credit reference rating score
Like a hoper on the pools awaiting draws
Store cards credit cards maxed out loan
Mortgaged to the hilt in a balsa wood home
Coca cola a burger in a bun
Coffin nail chips free for everyone
Get online download don't miss
Hurry to the fast food outlet

Lazy attitude piling on the pounds
These are the only ones you will ever have clown
Typing on the face book and other cyber wank
No opinions on the worlds affairs your vacant your blank
Play station in your underpants fifteen hours a day
No romance with the wife whilst this level's, here to play

Out with his so-called mates flashing cash he hasn't got
Delusions he's someone so is it money well spent?
Your washing's out it's raining your pants are on the line
That interview you thought you had is at a different place and time
….read your letter properly
Kitchen sink is full of pots bin open brims with waste
Next time you go shopping it's for paper cups and plates

Bus clippy

White hair starched shirt uniformed grey
Dreading the time quarter past three
When the school run is on its way
It all goes frantic at that time of day
Teenage school kids who play the fool
He's a different generation but of the same gene pool
Devoid of humour, with old fashioned views
All the kids are upstarts create too much fuss
"Sit down" he roars at the back of the school bus
Upstairs there's a rout as he insisted for full fare
So out came the sharpeners for the seats to tear

Slashed Ripped Damaged

Kids are still smoking which sends him into a rage
He's not collecting any fares he don't know who has paid
As they've ripped in half tickets and began to chew
He finds himself accusing pointing you you you
Switch seats dodge him pinch him for a dare
Upping the street creed amongst your peers
Memories that'll last you numerous years
They ridicule mock him like a music hall crowd
Targeting his badges neatly fastened on his lapel
Time to get shirty as kids try to give him hell
"Anymore fares"
"Anymore fares please?" On the bottom or the top
No matter his shouts No matter how loud
Horrible teens play big in their crowd
"Anymore fares" As the conductor comes round
Or just more abuse we are destination bound

Dolly

Heard a heartbeat some decades ago
Voices through the telly
Childs party ghostly movements
Shivers from the jelly
Call Draw! Like in a western
Fastest leaves his mark
No one can defend us
Reach out in the dark
Scramble amongst clothes jumbled
Book from a bygone age
Lies there all thrashed

Lacquered face scrapped to plaster
Squeaker long forgot or long squeezed out
Hands with missing fingers
Suited velvet worn to cloth
Link lines with vigorous scribbles
Mixed layers of childhood paints
Dolly seeks revenge for damage on its face
Its arms might seem limp
But a pen held tight….in hand

Came alive to reap havoc
Revenge of doll is planned
To draw write scribble
Mark make without fuss
Wants to follow facial contours
With an acid dipped brush
Scythe like action an urge to scribble your face
Damaged doll seeks owner for recompense
Whilst left to rot in attic dark
Over decades spent…Draw!

He wrote it in pen

He's got his mother's cheque book
So now he's on the phone
Ask for a mate to visit
Coz there's nobody at home
Bring your pencils with
You were goanna make our mark
Practice your handwriting
We've gotta make a start

If he gets caught he'll call it a loan
Cold be sent his brothers
If he's kicked out of home
But when if
He gets there
He'll be left in the dark
Throwing up stones for a way to get in
Like the wolf and the pigs
Chin chinney chin chin

Banging on the door from the cold outside
Crying through the letterbox
It's me…don't hide
I know that you're in there
I know that you're in there

The cheque books empty just fill in the blank
We'll cash it in the high street keep away from the bank
They charge a percentage that I don't mind

Sweaty palms are shaking
Tremble a bit
Smile at the lady wish for it
Per-ching goes the till the cheques rung in handed over in paper…
Twenty and tens alright

The trembles a jig now from left to the right
One hundred two hundred
To his delight
Were goanna have a fabulous night!

He'll soon get caught make no mistake

Under the covers he copied and traced
And he practiced and he practiced a whole month long like you do when you're learning the latest new song

Shoe be do be
Shoe be do be
Shoe be do be do ah shoe be do be
Shoe be do be do ah

He's got it all perfect so perfectly neat
So he cashed in some more cheques
But he wrote it in pen
He didn't use a pencil or a wax crayon

He needs the money but he dare not ask
So sorry mother I've run out of cash!
All that I've earned I've gambled away
Or drank it
Or lost it
In a stupid arsed way

He's sorry he's sorry
He's cashed in the book
Till it had gone empty
Just stubs left
Look
Lend us

Attack of the killer Prawn

The killer prawn rose from the sea unannounced
Like an erection from a giant Sea Urchin
Spitting salted bile at Fishermen crouched in terror
As their Boat rocks like a bath toy before bedtime

As the Prawn moves in for the kill
Its tail creates waves the height of abandoned tower blocks packed with dynamite ready to boom
Cracking the Boat to matchstick proportions.

Ship's crew destined as appetizers
For the creatures of the deep…. devouring flesh.
It's A million onto one!
As they swim in directional change without notice

Killer prawn
Like a fifty foot rubber gloved hand Waterproofed and deadly
Sinks trawler where its nets once dragged the sea bed.

Written for Tezza punky Prawn from the ESO.

Aliens lament

The tripods and Quadra pods
Crash-landed onto earth
Plunged into darkness
Deep-water sea. Feeding on flesh of Octopus
Did space ship 23
Mutated due to food that didn't agree if they were human
It would have been Burps
For aliens that landed it was made worse
The Mutation began with seventeen legs
Growths on their shoulders that soon become heads
They seek a launch pad to help fly them away.
From this planet called earth where their moon last a day.
Unknown to us humans
Our great Planet Earth to aliens in fact
Our planets, nothing but dirt.
Mass pollution, famine and wars
Greed slavery stuck in the pours were just a shelter
Like that for a bus
Littered grafftied that some aliens miss
Barren cold stinking of piss
These aliens crash landed had not intended to come
The universe out there fathoms of mass
Our planet's a pimple on the back of its ass

Hero was always villainous

Hero turns villain in the public eyes
Secrets untold are realised
Allegations speculations of the traumatised
Childhood hero evil to the marrowbone
In our homes appearing via goggle box
How the millions wrote sat and watched
Perceptions altered caught found out

Air Swimming

You've been black balled sonny
There's no other way
Just tilter on the edge
In the wind
Swaying
Don't look down
It'll make you sick
It wouldn't take long to go splat
But what would you recall
In the moment before that?
Was he pushed?
He didn't fall
Perhaps he tripped
There is no one up there
There was no one up there
Did he jump then?
Or was he
Caught by the wind
Then dropped like a stone…fer-ummmm
Then nothing…so quick
Air swimming
The frantic actions of the last moments of life
And he's air swimming
Or trying to gulp all the invisible marshmallows he can
With both arms
It's fear on his face or shock or what?
Too late
If you didn't notice
Should I call an ambulance or am I wasting my time

Just past my die by date

Prepared, watch synced
To do things you need to do
Allowing more time
Don't waste it ironing or hoovering then
Leave the pots in the bowl unwashed
Spend it wisely
Listening to your favourite vinyl 45rpm's
Dancing with a loved one
Or trampoline with the kids
This is no rehearsal
Approaching your final moments
As only, you know the secret
How did you find out?
Prophecy told me so
Within the pages of an old book
Found in a box on a car boot sale
Somewhere out in the sticks
Where only you visit for picnics

I had dreamed of Vampires

I had dreamed of Vampires
Lost in nightmares dark, when I awoke
I was that Vampire
I was there
It was I the Vampire that tasted Neck
It was me

Tell me

Tell me the worst mistake you made in your life
That you just can't take back
Tell me how you would feel if it was broadcast all over the news
So that everyone knew
Tell me how you would react to that

Tell me how you can change the world or how you would like things to be from here in
Tell me about you
I will not judge

South Bay Trash

No Grand hotel
Just B and B
Holiday time family
If the weather holds good
Part success
Let's take the bus to the south bay trash
Two pence slots atm cashed
Fish and chips cooked up in beef fat
Candy floss seafood trade
Plastic buckets lemonade
Trinkets towels coloured rock
Policeman's hats joke shop props
Sounds of brass across the bay
Surf and sand
Holiday

Wishing

Come, we are going to play
With your emotions
Through the eyes of a Child
Wanting

The first child well fed, loved
Doesn't need no stuffed bear
With a heart n' wishes
"Oh Daddy. It's so cute. This one, buy it for me."

The second child is starving
Doesn't know where her next meal is coming from
Mother is that weak she can't breastfeed her young infant
She too has a wish

survival

Wonder boy and the Pig

Out there oink
Wonder boy turns, faces the people
But no mask
He's fresh not like MacLean's
But in his own way as fresh as he's goanna get.
What's his game? Loyalty?
The creep
To eat at the top table?

Why do we ask wonder boy does as he does?
Throwing caution to the wind
In his stupidity or ignorance or both
He is too self-important
Wonder boy knows nothing
Never will, can't compute

Poop trees

Someone hung a bag from a tree
At eye level, white testicals hang knotted intensely
I notice them more as I drive or walk streets or country lanes
Poop trees everywhere
Hanging bag of waste quivers in the wind
Dog owners reluctant to carry home and dispose of
Humans in need caught out
Decorate the poop tree
But don't tell a soul.

Pub auction

Make no mistake
If they get caught...robbin'
In houses flats on our estate from families
With little or shit stuff to rake in
It'll be you...who's gettin' broken
Do the math's nothing into nothing
Just don't go mate.
Flymo's for three (in the green). Four (Mr... You)
Commission bid
Wanna bike - bid five
Sky box without the box, Six no instruction manual
Remote damaged, sellotaped scratched
Any takers (seven)
They used to empty their sheds and lofts
Before burglar's came about
Down at the pub auctions
For something they could tout
It was a social event
A place to meet a bargain to be had
Pint of beer with a splash
A deal struck good or bad
Auction for the car boot
Buy and take them away
If it's smashed or damaged
Sell it back as miss... with
Stuck together magazines
Toys that smell of piss
About making money
(How much could you make?)
Barter as "collectable"
Persuade antique
Okay it might be broken
Had it for weeks...months in fact
Interested? (Eight) women in the blue
Commission out, do I have twelve
Estate sheds empty some flats and houses too...
Televisions without remote controls, a pair of glass cockatoos
Box of broken give away's, photo albums from the seal
Auction for the car boot
Comes soon to your estate when it does let hope
The robberies don't start here mate.

The Shoe Queen

Imelda had many shoes
Whilst people went hungry
She could not decide
If to wear the buckle strap or high heels
Decisions decisions

Comic book anti hero

He's your comic book anti hero
His kisses are his weapons
They taste you see
Taste of after save…and sick
Yeah, they like the sweet smell
That's what gets 'em
The sweet sweet smell…drawing 'em in
The net has been cast
And all you have to do now is just wait…
The lips connect and as tongues entwine…the kiss turns to choke
And the vomit rushes …..**WHAM!**
Both mouths full….. And filling
The aftershave was not used as scent
He drank it like meths
That was **HIS** choice
His rules his agenda…his habit
Sorry I got sick…it won't happen again
Forgive me
Let's wipe our mouths
Clean our teeth
Start again please.

Quirky little hook

This is a business, a big business set up to make one thing. Money.
Advertisements in and on the back of magazines
On line, in the media, down our streets on large billboards that never make us smile or laugh are everywhere.
With constantly changing visuals that seem suggestive, seed planting, and look nice. I don't want your advice nor does quirky little hook whose only job was to try to reel the public in.

It's just a sales pitch
If I need something I hope I can afford it.
No hard sell please
Telephone Sales people are not welcome, sorry
I did say sorry, now hang up before me.
Yes, I know it's just a job. On commission are we?
I just don't like the hard sell. You don't know me.

Like chuggers in the street. Avoid eye contact at all cost
No: I don't need a cooling off period
Price or quality price or quality what's it to be
Good after sales have it on the nod pay nothing for years
Just sign here
Jobs a good UN

R five

Standing at the window
Waiting for the bus
I hope it's a full one
I wanna cause some fuss
Up with the Venetians standing' in me skin
Hoping for the travellers to have a gander in
R Five R Five look through the gl'arse R Five
Now I am standing naked can you see my arse?

Having the timetable
I never knew could be such fun
I know when the bus arrives
Not like anyone
I'll remove my clothing and wave to everyone
Coz the bus stops right outside my house
R Five R Five

I don't mind the neighbours or shoppers that I meet
Sometimes there's total strangers standing in the street
They'll always say hello to me
But please don't call the police
Coz I'm just about to surprise some bus travellers
R Five R Five look through the gl'arse R Five
R Five R Five look through the gl'arse R Five
Now I'm at me window
Do you wanna see me arse?

Shops gone

Too late……….shops gone
Too late should have used that one
TOO LATE SHOP CLOSED DOWN
No Bargains
No Sale
No Customers……….
Where were you
When it was open?

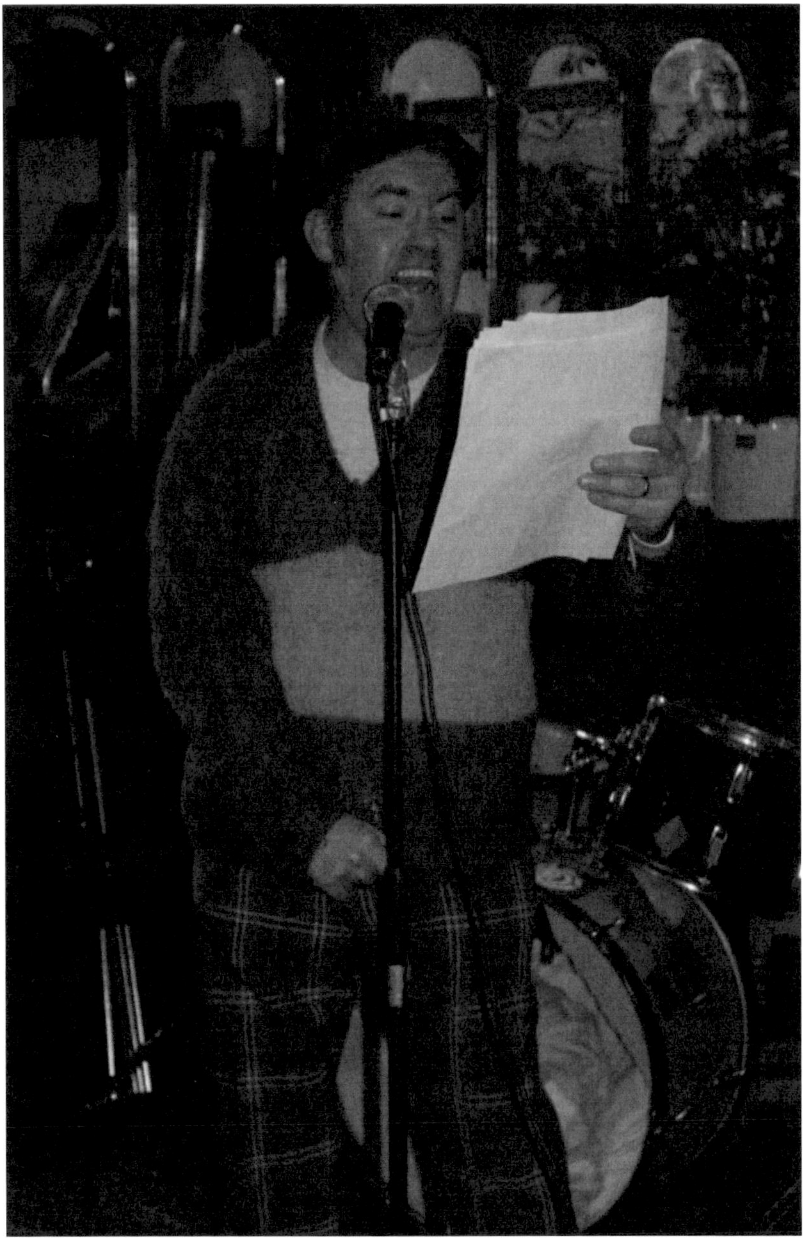

Arrive Dachau (Death)

In the final hour I shall come
And set the sun
Scattering at your heels
In those days
With no warning I shall come
Expect no long farewell
It shall be swift.

Written September 1986

Keep away from me

You've read my e-mails
Before me
You have my pictures in a gallery
You seek some self-pity
You're a stalker (baby)
Keep away from me

I've not wrote,
It's not me who wants to find
I don't play hide and seek
Not now or never
You're a stalker baby (keep away from me)

See a doctor
Let him get inside your head
Inside your mind
Maybe…he can seek…
What it is you want to find
You're a stalker baby (keep away from me)

As long as it's not me baby.

Yellow pages you're the spy
Drowning in a sea of E files
You're a stalker baby (KAFM)
You seem to have hung onto the past
Well I don't keep a diary
Never have
You're a stalker baby (KAFM)

You're fed… your life's… Shit

Fed all this shit via sky TV the newspaper group
With their slant on society
Coupon gives always their all in Cahoots
Check your credit reference-rating thing
Print it off to find out what you bought
What it was that you could not afford
Or never had growing up, and are still without as an adult

Free Coca Cola a burger in a bun coffin nail chips
Free for everyone, get on line and download do not miss…

Getting lazy attitude piling on the pounds these are the only ones you will ever have clown
Typing on the face book and other cyber wank
No opinions on the world's affairs no please nor thanks
Play station in the underpants fifteen hours a day
No children yet is he firing blanks or no time in the day

You have washing out its raining your pants are on the line
The interview you thought you had is at a different time
Kitchen sink is full of pots bin open brims with waste
Next time I go shopping it's for paper cup & plates

Drunk

His walk stutters as he almost tripped himself that time
Swaying from one side to another
He's drunk
Smashed
Avoidable

His stagger has no strut
There is no swagger
Just a balancing act
Without the wire
Without the net
Keep off the road
There are dangers there
Nobody matters… nobody cares
If he falls

He's drunk
Smashed
Avoidable

You're not eighteen anymore

You know you can listen to Nick Heyward on the radio
Haircut one hundred
Yes you can listen to Nick Heyward on the radio
It doesn't have to be punk rock all the time
Do you understand?
You're not eighteen anymore
It doesn't matter
You spend the time doing what you wanna do
If you had the time
You pay your bills now
You pay them
You pay your bills
You look after your things
You're not eighteen anymore
You're not eighteen anymore
Do you understand?
                                      Yeh I know I know it
It doesn't matter
It just doesn't matter
You don't have to be punk rock anymore
You haven't got any hair left to dye
It's gone
It's fallen out
It's over
You can wear some of the clothes that's ok
But they don't fit you anymore
You've sort of err outgrown them Yeh out grown them

Druggie on the roof

You won't catch him that's our dad
He's given you run around…drove you mad
He's clever… whilst you are the fool
Nothing can hold him... he don't use rules
Why don't you go away leave him be
Mother's making dinner and it's pizza for tea
Let us back in …
Give us the keys t' 'ouse
Come on copper stop muckin' about

Up through the attic break out on the roof
Straddle along the ridge tiles wave to the group
…gathering… in the streets below
Here's some tiles copper
Now watch them go

Rush get a deck chair
Go down the local shop
Twenty fags for mother
There's a man on top
Of a rooftop
Look Look over there

Also get some crisps any flavour will do
And if there's some change get some tinnies too
Don't hang about…there's one in it for you

So he rushed back as the kids are off school
Texting his mates to watch the neighbour hood fool
Bikes and hoodies all over the place
Road taped off Police line don't break

Yes there's commotion on our estate
The old uns put their teeth in watch and wait
See the copter as it circles round?
Relaying information to the police on the ground
There's an ambulance fireman too
It's a nice afternoon the weathers improved

A reporter, local news
Gathering information via neighbours views
Photographer she looks nice
How's about a picture of me and the wife?
No school run? Unless he comes down
Young kids arrested for feeding this clown

You can't catch him are the young kids taunts
Even though his house is a regular haunt
Take him out quick with a shot from a gun
Forget about coaxing or upsetting someone

There are plenty here that will do it
Just for fun
Aim
Fire
Game over
Job done
There's an agency job now on the go
Cleaning the street after the show
A twelve hour shift minimum wage
Month in hand before you get paid
Don't you want it?
Who wants it?
Anybody?
Bring your own brush

MELBOURNE FEST
DERBYSHIRE

DWANE READS... POETRY.

15th + 16th SEPT 2012
SAT   SUN

12 NOON CASTLE HOUSE
1PM RUSSELLS YARD
2PM MELBOURNE ASSEMBLY ROOMS

INFO: dwanereads@gmail.com

Muston Conway

Muston Conway
The cowboy star is a fraud
Wigged suited and booted
Nothing of his own making
Such a let down
When we found out.

Unicorn Tales

By day, he worked putting the holes in cheese
When he wasn't an extra in My Little Pony
Or
It was endless auditions for storybook tales

Sorry but unicorns don't exist

The sugar candy world of make believe
Is what it is - fantasy
Please don't tell the children

Thanks page

Firstly, Dave Hill the bloke who used to take my school dinner money in exchange for some wonderful vinyl all those years ago at RE.Cords. (Now BPM). **This is your entire fault**. John Cooper Clarke gig c/o raw promotions (Alan & Lisa Wooley). Johnny Vincent. Wonderful gigs over the years. Jon Hodgson. Help with "Rough Guts" Feb 2012. Danny Tua. For support over the years, with various gigs including Performance Art. Eagle spits and Rachel Eagling for some fantastic gigs in some great venues, always positive, a great couple. **Please make sure you support Punk for the Homeless gigs**. Jennie Russell Smith. Rebellion Festival.Blackpool.2012. (Poetry in the Spanish Hall). Steve Walker, Buxton festival Fringe. HCE. Adam Steiner and Gary Sykes- Blythe. For believing in my poetry work & publishing some of it. Trevor Tomlin (Sheffield Sharrow festival 2013).

Helen Brailsford. (Melbourne Festival). Leon Lenny Pwosion Hodgetts. (Intake club Mansfield). Gary White. Sitwell Tavern. Derby. Jonny March. For some great gigs. Thanks mate, up the ESO! **DIY POETS NOTTINGHAM.** Frank McMahon. Clare Stewart. Miggy Angel. John Humphreys. Jim Willis. Marty Everett. Eagle Spits. Rachel Eagling. A. Sole. **ROMP. ROTHERHAM**. Gav Roberts. Carol Robson. Chris Bilton. Bob Roberts. Steve Williams. Bo Mason. Greg Muscroft. Sylvia D KittyFly. Christine May Turner.

Andrew Mark Bedell. Adam Morris. Wayne Palmer- Dyson. Addie P. Abbott. Plus, everyone else who goes to Romp.
SPOKEN WORLDS. Gary Carr. Karen Carr, Mal Dewhirst. Gary Longden. Margaret Thorr. Ian Ward. Tom Wrye. Ray & Terri Jolland. Bob Stevens. Word Wizards. (Buxton). Pete Hubbard.
SPIRE WRITES. Helen Mort. Matt McAteer. Melanie McAteer. Tony Keeton. Dave Attrill. Matt Black. River Walton.

DERBY QUAD POETS. Les Baynton. Jeremy Duffield. Rain. Duncan Fraser. Mark Cleaver, Andy Biddulph. Phil Binding. Jim Hall from the Mouthy Poets. Stephen Vaughan Williams. Lilly Gornall. Dave Wadsworth (Alfreton Pottery). **Photography**. Anthony Fisher (p6, 95). Hal Wright (p61, 79). Holly Monroe (p10, 17, 69). Julian Sewell of Black Factory Photography. (p98). Jane Stanton. (Lichfield poets). Matt McGuiness and Furthest from the sea team (Derby). Richard Young & John Wood (Tea for Two). Pip & Elaine Southall. Seema Gill & Richard Heley. (Piggyback publishing. Always encouraging, great Artist). Joolz Denby. Steve Pottinger. Neil Smith (film maker). Dave Costello. (Wirral Festival). Mickey Sheehan. Victoria Inn, Derby. **Richie Lock.** (Ska Soup). (The Ska r. Thanks for having my logo done on your car. Amazing!) Baz. At Doghouse. Carlton, Nottingham. Great gigs with, The Poor Geezers (put you in Dean and Rob), Kosmischeboy, Eaglespitshexx, Dark Valentine The Reverends, Wonk unit, Zooparty, Mr. Wolf, Crompton Thresher, Electric Shiite Orchestra, The Parents. James Carter-for the tees- Chesterfield Punk and Ska nights. Acorn Roots. (Adam, Dave, Leon & Owen). Adam Thompson, O Great Bear, Eddie Rose, Richard Hunter, Sods Law. (James thanks for putting me on at some great gigs). Exit the Network, Phil Taylor (PA Guy at Bunkers Hill). Propane 4, Bruce Tality, Birmingham Arts Festival team. Yaffle Café. Morledge, Derby. City Zine, All the Derby, Nottingham & Yorkshire Punks. Attila the Stockbroker. Alina Pendolina Airline (pic p84). Addictive Philosophy. Andrew Morton (promoter). Dave Fungalpunk HT. Words Escape me. Aka Jonathan Barrington. Steve 'noz' Norris. Nick Fenton (Apocalypse Babys). The Boston lot,

A Big Thanks goes out to anyone who bought some Merch & of course, for spending the money to buy this book. Dwane Reads

www.dwanereadspoetry.weebly.com

Bookings and further information dwanereads@gmail.com

You write a poem now.

(About something from this book)

Send it to

theannoyingmegaphonepigeon@hotmail.co.uk

Thank you

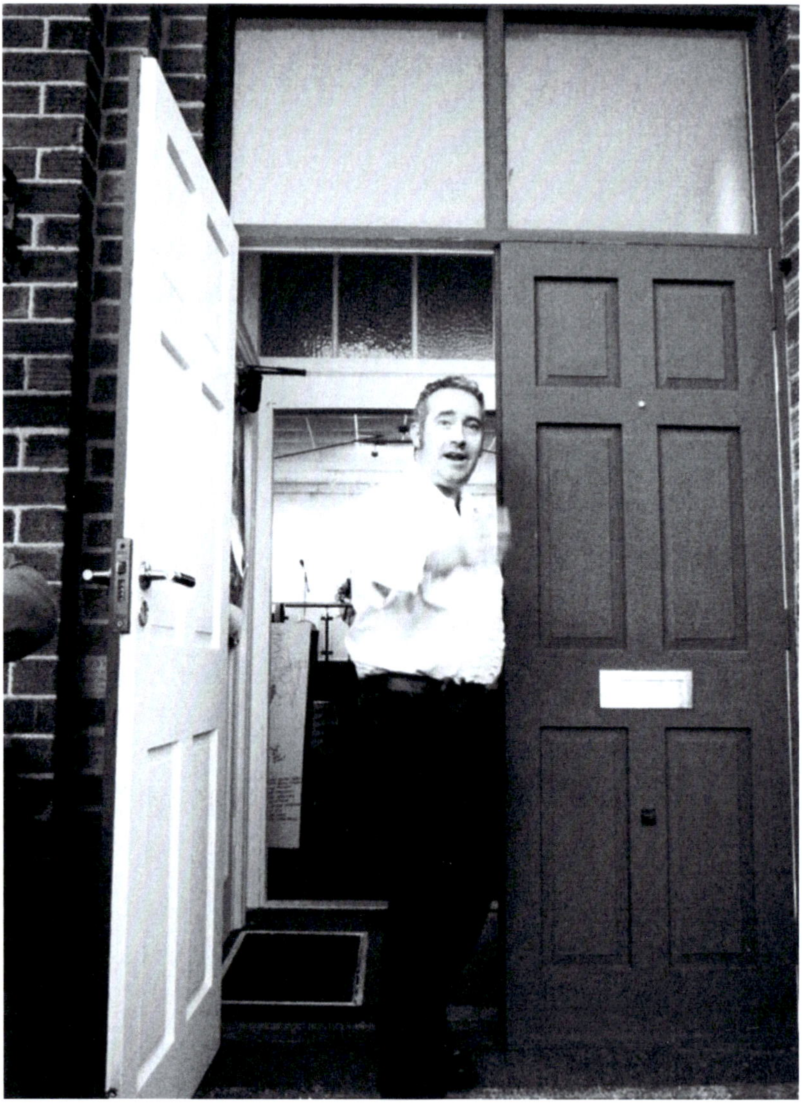